THE **TESTING** SERIES

THE **ULTIMATE** AIRLINE SELECTION AND INTERVIEW PREPARATION GUIDE

BY LEE WOOLASTON

THE **TESTING** SERIES
expert advice on test preparation

how2become

Orders: Please contact How2become Ltd, Suite 2, 50 Churchill Square Business Centre, Kings Hill, Kent ME19 4YU.
Please order via the email address info@how2become.co.uk.

ISBN: 9781907558658

First published 2012

Typeset for How2become Ltd by Molly Hill, Canada.

Printed in Great Britain for How2become Ltd by Bell & Bain Ltd, 303 Burnfield Road, Thornliebank, Glasgow G46 7UQ.

CONTENTS

DISCLAIMER AND COPYRIGHT NOTICE

INTRODUCTION

I would like to thank you very much for buying the guide and congratulate you on getting an airline assessment. If you haven't got one yet, I'm sure that you will do soon if you follow the advice contained in this guide.

At the time of writing we are in the midst of a global recession. Things will certainly turnaround within a few years and then the airline pilot job market will be manic. However, jobs are still plentiful in the Middle East, Asia and in the Far East. With aircraft orders higher than ever, and the pilot workforce requirement forecast to double within the next 20 years (Boeing), the future promises to be bright for pilots. I recently heard the chief pilot of a major airline quote the number 465,000 as the required number of pilots in the next 18 years.

I would like to briefly introduce myself and give you a glimpse of my career so far in Aviation. I am currently a Captain with a Major UK Regional Airline. I fly the Embraer 135/145 at present, a modern regional passenger jet airliner. I have approaching 5000 flying hour's total time (3500 with the airlines) and I hold a JAA ATPL.

My interest in learning to fly started when I did a series of parachute jumps for cancer research. After answering lots of my questions, the pilots at the parachute club said that it would be a good idea if I stopped "bugging" them and booked myself a trial-flying lesson. That is exactly what I did and the rest, as they say, is history. I was hooked from the off-set and instinctively knew that this was what I wanted to do for a living. It is interesting that every pilot I have ever asked the question – "how did you get in to flying?" always has a unique story to tell.

I became a flying instructor ten years ago (at the time of writing) and eight years ago I landed my first job as an airline pilot. Within eighteen months I had progressed to a major regional UK Airline where I have spent the last six and a half years. I achieved my Command Level eighteen months ago and I have really enjoyed my career so far.

It is my intention within this guide to give you a **good idea** of the type of assessments that you will likely undergo when you get called for your selection day(s). Each Airline selection process is different, ranging from some airlines having a "chat" and a simulator assessment, all the way through to those airlines that do a 2/3-day detailed assessment with a combination of the tests covered in this guide. (You will probably find lots of information about your particular assessment on www.pprune.com, which is a pilot forum). Within this guide however, I will take you through the entire process, from application forms, CV's and covering letters to examples of all of the typical assessments and interviews

Just a few points about application forms – most of them are now completed online, and as mentioned in my last guide "How2become an Airline Pilot", in the UK a lot of "newbie" applications will be made to companies such as CTC Wings, Oxford Aviation Academy and FTE Jerez prior to commencement of training.

Typically there will be some essay type questions; make sure you keep things to the point and direct. For example, if the question says "briefly describe" do not waffle on endlessly. I recommend that you also watch out for phrases such as "most difficult" in application form questions. Many people fail to keep their answer specific and as a result they fail to get their application through.

Before submitting your form you should also carry out a thorough spelling and grammar check of your work and get someone sensible to check your answers.

READ THE INSTRUCTIONS CAREFULY

Remember the abbreviations RTFQ! (Read the *Flippin'* Question) and always complete the questions carefully. I would estimate that 50% of applications are "kicked out" because of a failure to follow the reasons above. Make sure yours isn't one of them.

There are still plenty of Airlines that accept the *old fashioned*, CV and Covering Letter. Because of this fact I will be covering them during the next chapter.

CHAPTER 1
THE CV AND COVERING LETTER

You will have gone through a tremendous amount of time and effort with your training so you owe it to yourself to spend a decent amount of time on your CV and covering letter. I have enclosed a sample Covering Letter and CV at the end of this chapter to assist you. The following guidelines will also help you:

1ST TOP TIP

Always include a recent/professional photo with your CV application. A head and shoulders shot in the top right hand corner should be sufficient. Remember, the photo will probably be the first thing that attracts their attention, so make sure it's professional and presentable. Otherwise your CV could end in the rubbish bin.

2ND TOP TIP

Never send a solo CV (unless specifically requested). Prepare a well-written covering letter. This will act as an "Advert" for your CV. Use this letter to emphasise skills that set you apart from your peers. I will be writing more about this subject later in the chapter with an example.

3RD TOP TIP

Make sure there are no grammatical errors or spelling mistakes in your CV.

4TH TOP TIP

You stand a better chance if you tailor your CV to the airline you
are applying for. This will involve some research on your part whilst
constructing your CV.

5TH TOP TIP

Your CV should not be longer than one or two pages. Try to remember that
it is a life summary, not your autobiography.

6TH TOP TIP

Try not to use a font smaller than 10 points and avoid using fancy font types.
Just stick to one standard type such as Arial or Times New Roman. Finally, I
recommend you avoid coloured paper.

7TH TOP TIP

Avoid using negative expressions, such as, "unfortunately," "no experience" etc.

8TH TOP TIP

Make sure there are no gaps in your CV. (For example, in your work history
try to provide a seamless timespan of employment). If there have been
times when you have been unemployed due to studying or training, be sure
to state this in your CV. Period's during your professional life spent doing
voluntary or community work are also positive aspects to add to your CV.
You will need to prove your history for the last 5 years; otherwise you will
not get a UK Airport Security Pass. My Airline had to fire a new entrant First
Officer recently, because he couldn't prove his last 5 years work history. It
turned out that he'd made it all up!

9TH TOP TIP

Before sending your CV, get someone to proofread it carefully. You may
decide to pay a professional proofreader to do this work for you.

10TH TOP TIP

Avoid sending your CV in a hand-written envelope. All modern printers are able to cope with printing on envelopes. This is a chance for you to discover buttons on your printer you never knew existed!

Note: It seems acceptable in the industry that including a photo is less important nowadays, especially as many application forms require a copy of your passport, driving licence etc. Also if you have a degree, then do you really need to include GCSE/ A levels etc.? You could save a lot of space this way.

CV STRUCTURE

"Your CV is a concise and handy summary of your flying credentials and will often be used by the interviewers during the interview."

As I mentioned earlier, your airline pilot CV is very different to the "every day" stuff. It will need to be written specifically with flying in mind. So, it's a good idea to include any management, leadership or relevant technical skills from previous employment. Your flying story to date should be clearly mapped out.

YOUR CV WILL GENERALLY CONSIST OF 6 HEADINGS:

1. **Personal Details:** Contact details, nationality, availability, relocation, status.

2. **Flying Qualifications and Experience:** under this heading you should state where you trained, the type of licence and rating you possess i.e. Frozen ATPL, EASA CPL/IR and also the total flying times; Twins, Singles, MCC and JOC etc. Next, mention your ratings i.e. Instructor Rating and other relevant qualifications.

3. **General Education:** All the way from high school including any college/university education etc.

4. **Languages:** Here you can mention your 'mother tongue' and detail any fluent or conversational languages.

5. **Career Summary:** Under this heading provide details of your career to date. You will have to explain any gaps as previously discussed. Remember, do not be dishonest. You have to prove your last 5 years minimum.

6. **Interests and Achievements:** I.e. Gliding, ballooning, charity work etc.

THE COVERING LETTER

Try to keep this letter short and to the point. It is the tool you can use to introduce your CV. Use a conversational writing style and avoid using the word "I" too much. Let's look at the typical structure of a cover letter:

THE HEADING

This should consist of your contact details, name, address, telephone number and email address. Leave your MSN or Skype name out.

THE RECEIVER

A letter addressed to a person makes a better impression. So, try to find out the name of the recruiter. You may find this information on **www.pilotjobsnetwork.com**, on the Airlines website or a pilot forum such as **www.pprune.com**. Finally, you could ring up the company's switchboard and ask the operator for the name of the person who deals with recruitment. Make sure though, that you get the correct spelling, otherwise your efforts could end up in vain.

For a list of every AOC (Air Operator Certificate) holder in the UK, including every UK Airline, large and small, please visit **www.caa.co.uk/aocholders**

You can then use **www.pilotjobsnetwork.com** or **www.pprune.com** to find out the contacts, criteria etc.

THE FIRST PARAGRAPH

This should state clearly the reason you are writing to xyz Airline. Two or three sentences will be sufficient. Also, state your objective and that you have enclosed (or attached, in the case of email) your CV.

THE BODY

In this section you can highlight the desired pilot profile of the airline. Tell the recruiter the flying experience you have and how it may be relevant to the role you are applying for, i.e. some Airlines seem to prefer **Integrated Students** whilst some seem to prefer **Flying Instructors** trained at Oxford etc. Make sure you point this out to them in the body of your letter.

THE CLOSING PARAGRAPHS

Close your letter with a statement promoting you as a strong, capable candidate for the position. The close should contain a discreet request for action, such as – "I look forward to meeting you in the near future," or "please forward an application form." Finish off by signing your name personally with a contrasting ink colour.

Just in case you are having problems coming up with those perfect phrases for your cover letter, I have compiled a helpful list of specific pilot cover letter phrases that will assist you in writing an effective covering letter:

"I am writing to express interest in a position as..."

"Your company's reputation as the most punctual regional airline has prompted me..."

"Enclosed for your review is my CV which briefly outlines my experience and education"

"I would welcome the opportunity to..."

"Solid career progression"

"For more than five years I have flown extensive _____ operations"

"I have extensive experience..."

"The following are highlights of my qualifications..."

"My experience includes..."

"Relevant to your needs, I offer: (bullet points follow these phrases)"

"Your company's exciting new fleet of _____"

"My greatest strength (asset) is..."

"I am confident that my experience and education to date provide me with the skills that would benefit your airline."

"My experience, professionalism, and enthusiasm..."

"I am confident that my background in flying _____ makes me a qualified candidate for your First Officer position."

"I would like to meet with you and discuss my skills and background and how they would contribute to your company's needs."

"I offer strong team leadership and effective communication skills."

"I'm excited about the future of XYZ Air and am eager to contribute to its growth."

"Thank you for your consideration. I look forward to hearing from you."

Before I finish this chapter, I would like to draw your attention to a supportive organisation that would be well worth joining. It is called British Airline Pilots Association (BALPA). You will find them at: **www.balpa.org** and it's free to join if you are a student pilot. You will receive lots of current information about airline contacts, recruitment procedures and interview advice, CV writing tips and salaries. Every year they organise a recruitment conference, where representatives from almost all airlines in Britain are present. This can give you the added benefit of meeting up and talking with them about their current recruitment plans.

There is also the **Flyer Magazine Annual Professional Flight Training Exhibition**, which has many UK Airlines and FTO's in attendance. In the words of the event organisers, it's an "Absolute must for anyone considering a career as a professional Pilot". I have heard nothing but praise for this event!

Over the next few pages I have enclosed a sample Covering Letter and a sample CV to give you a rough guide.

SAMPLE COVERING LETTER

I Wannabe
320, Airbus Rd
Chester
CTR 321

0321 340380

27 May 2012

Captain Fred Bloggs
Chief Pilot
XYZAIR
Bristol
Somerset
UW ARR

Dear Captain Bloggs,

I am applying for the position of First Officer on the Airbus A319, which was advertised in Flight International dated 26 May – 02 June 2012 reference XYZAIR/A319.

My ambition has been to work for XYXAIR ever since my work experience with the airline from 2010 to 2011 inclusive. Since then I have continued to monitor the airline's progress and have been impressed by its high standards, customer focus and effective marketing strategy, which has resulted in its load factors increasing in the midst of a global recession.

I hold an EASA Frozen ATPL gained at XYZ Flight Training and I am also MCC and JOT qualified on the A319. I gained first time passes in the CPL and IR flight tests. I also passed all of the EASA Exams first time averaging 90%.

I am available now and I'm willing to relocate as required; please find enclosed my CV.

Yours Sincerely,

I Wannabe

CURRICULUM VITAE – IMAR WANNABE

Personal Details:
320, Airbus Rd
Chester
CTR 321

Mobile 0747 321319
Telephone 0321 340380
Email: I_wanabe@me.com
Nationality: Bristolian

Availability: immediate
Date of Birth: 01/01/90
Relocate: As required
Status: Single

Flying Qualifications and Experience

March 2011 to June 2012 EASA Frozen ATPL at XYZ Flight Training School
Full first time pass in CPL and IR skills tests
Total Flying 307 hrs: 40 hrs PA34 150 hrs PA28 – PPL 117 hrs
Total Sim 78 hrs: 15 hrs MCC, 25 hrs JOC (A319) and 33 hrs (PA34)
PPL, Hot Air Ballooning 25 hrs and Gliding 150 hrs

General Education:

2007 – 2010 2.1 Physics at University of Birmingham
2005 – 2007 4 'A' Levels: Physics, Maths, English and French, Bristol College
2001 – 2005 9 GCSE at 'C' and above: Brunel School, Bristol

Languages:

English – Mother tongue, French – Fluent, German – Conversational.

Career Summary:

Part-time employment whilst in full time education to help fund Flight Training.

2007 – 2010 Assistant Manager. Restaurant Staff at Mcdonalds Bristol, responsible for 8 staff, rostering, purchasing, accounts, interviewing and training

2002 – 2007 Voluntary Worker. Bristol Gliding Club, assisting in scheduling, operations, ground lectures. Organised the annual dinner and dance raised £950.

Interests and Achievements:

Warrant officer in ATC, First Solo at 16 and gained PPL at 17, captained my county Rugby Union team, organised a 4 week bicycle ride across India raising £2000 for charity. Duke of Edinburgh Gold award while at college.

CHAPTER 2
PREPARING FOR YOUR INTERVIEW

FIRST IMPRESSION

"It's a little known fact that the majority of interviewers make up their mind about you in the first two minutes!"

PREPARE, PREPARE, PREPARE! Candidates who attend an interview often under achieve, simply because they do not prepare themselves fully. There is no particular format for an interview; some are very formal and can take well over an hour with three or more people, whilst others are far less formal with one or two people and take 15 – 20 minutes to complete. It is better to be fully prepared for the worst case than to be under-prepared.

TYPICAL AREAS THAT ARE ASSESSED AND SCORED DURING THE AIRLINE PILOT INTERVIEW ARE:

Personal – Academic, non-academic, sporting interests and achievements, personal domestic situation.

Team Skills – Team, leader and followership skills experience. Interpersonal relationships.

Flying – Training, where, when and what grades, experience, knowledge of company, from initial to present, since qualifying.

Technical – Theory of flight, performance and systems. I recommend you buy *Ace the Technical Pilot Interview* by Gary. V. Bristow, *Preparing for your Cathay Pacific Interview* by Captains X, Y and Z, and *Handling The Big Jets* by D.P. Davies. You should also concentrate on the questions in this guide.

Communications – verbal, non-verbal, voice projection, eye contact, psychometric tests.

Impression – Including attitude to all members of staff, punctuality, appearance, enthusiasm, manner, bearing and motivation.

I would recommend that you carry out an interview preparation course on a one-to-one basis with a professional that can guarantee *real* results. Email me (ONLY IF YOU HAVE AN INTERVIEW PLEASE) at **frozenatpl@aol.co.uk** and I will give you the details of a person who I recommend.

This particular person has helped hundreds of people get through interviews successfully, *including me!* They have knowledge of most UK Airlines' interview requirements. Your weaknesses will be very quickly spotted and corrected, i.e. eye contact, handshake, under confident, nervous mannerisms etc.

Use **www.ppjn.com** in addition to **www.pprune.com** to find out any info regarding the interview or the "gouge" as it is called. Check the company website for company news and 'Google' them to see what else there is to know about them.

Finally, network, network, network! Make an effort to establish new *flying* contacts and friends and find out what they know about the company you are applying for. Use social media, Facebook Twitter, MySpace, LinkedIn etc.

ANALYSE YOURSELF

Be prepared to summarise your life (particularly your flying career to date). Use the Non-Technical questions in this guide to assist you. For example, what, when and why for becoming a pilot, why do you want to work for this company and don't forget your weaknesses, strengths, highs and lows etc. Where do you want to be in the short, medium and long term? What do you have to offer the company?

I will be covering the Technical interview in another section of this guide, but if you haven't already done so, buy the following books and study them before attending your interview:

Ace the Technical Pilot Interview by Gary V Bristow

Preparing for your Cathay Pacific Interview by Captains X,Y and Z.

Handling the Big Jets by D.P. Davies

CHAPTER 3
THE NON-TECHNICAL INTERVIEW (THIS IS WHERE MOST PEOPLE FALL DOWN)

After all the hard work of getting an interview, many people fall down during the Non-Technical interview. In this section it is my intention to give you a breakdown of the different Non-Technical skills and attributes that the Airlines are looking for, followed by lots of "typical" Non Tech' Questions, so that you can get a better idea of how to answer them.

In most cases you should strive to give a sensible and relevant answer of some sort. There will be a million and one answers to each type of question; it's just a case of staying calm and answering wisely, without digging a big hole!

TOP TIP – PAUSE, THINK AND THEN ANSWER...

I would strongly recommend that you practice and rehearse your answers to the questions within this chapter. Write your answers in pencil in the guide to help you prepare. I also recommend that you say the answers out loud enough times so that you sound natural and spontaneous. Before you start the Non-Technical Questions however, I have covered many of the required skills for the role of an Airline Pilot below. As you read through them, think about your own experiences and make a note.

THEY ARE LOOKING FOR:

- A strong positive attitude.
- A safety conscious attitude.
- Captain Potential – Airlines only ever employ future Captains!
- Somebody that performs well under stress/pressure.
- A team player.
- An ability to learn.
- Someone that looks, acts, dresses and speaks as a professional.
- A self-confident person- with a streak of humility.
- Someone that's well rounded and personable.
- Someone with an ability to influence other people without dominating them.
- Someone that is customer-oriented.
- Good ability to communicate.
- Able to facilitate, plan and organise.
- A good sense of humor.
- Ability to work with all types of people.
- Cost and profit aware.
- A role model.
- Past, present and future oriented.
- A love of flying.

LEADERSHIP AND MANAGEMENT:

With regard to leadership and management the Airlines require the following abilities/skills:

- To be able to inspire people with enthusiasm.
- To be approachable and visible.
- Motivate the team with appreciation.
- Change style as the situation changes.
- Show interest, empathy and respect.
- Team involvement and task completion.

STANDARDS:

- Compliance with rules.
- Intervene if task deviates from standard.
- Deviate from standards if situation requires it.

WORKLOAD:

- Tasks prioritised.
- Distribute workload appropriately.
- Allocate enough time.
- Authority and Assertiveness:
- Advocate own position.
- Take control if required.

PLANNING AND COORDINATION:

- Project ahead.
- Plan clearly shared and if necessary adapted.
- Make full use of all available resources and data.
- Encourage team participation in planning.
- Encourage review of progress of plan.

PROBLEM SOLVING AND DECISION MAKING:

There is an acronym that a lot of Airlines use for dealing with a problem called: DODAR.

D – Diagnosis – What has happened? Why has it happened?

O – Options – generate options

D – Decide – Decide on the best course of action

A – Allocate – Delegate duties, teamwork

R – Review – Is the plan working? If not start DODAR again.

TEAMWORK:

Group exercises will test the following:

- **Team building** – open participation environment, encourages feedback and does not compete.

- **Supporting others** – offering solution to problems, show genuine interest and praise where appropriate, assist other team members in demanding situations, tolerant of weaknesses.

- **Understand the team needs** – feedback, condition of crew-members, take notice of others' suggestions and listen without interrupting.

- **Conflict solving** – agreeing to disagree, admit own errors, concentrate on what is right, suggest solutions, keep calm, ability to de-escalate conflict.

BUSINESS AND CUSTOMER AWARENESS:

- **Business prioritisation** – acknowledges conflicting priorities and exercise sound judgment.

- **Customer focus** – provides timely and relevant flow of information to the passenger, promote the company when appropriate, apply appropriate behavior when dealing with customers.

- **Supporting other departments** – establish professional relationships with other departments.

- **Business understanding** – understands the impact on the business, identify reasons for profit/loss centres of the organisation.

COMPETENCY BASED INTERVIEWS

A few airline-interviewing panels are now using CBI (competency based interviews). Top marks will be given to answers containing PAR (Problem Action Result) whilst nil marks will be given if you can't think of an example! Marks are given for the amount of evidence and the quality of the example. You can ask to return to a question later – but you **MUST** answer it. It's vital that you answer all questions.

TELL A STORY

Each question that you will be asked is fishing for a particular concern. Before giving your answer don't be afraid to pause for 20/30 seconds before you respond. You need to deliver your response to ensure that you eliminate the concern of the interviewer.

When designing your own personal answers for many of the questions following shortly, use the following acronym "STORY" to respond by telling them a story!

S – Situation (brief outline)

T – Target (To be accomplished)

O – Organise (how you organised the required action)

R – Results (describe the outcome)

Y - Why (y)? (Tell them why they needn't be concerned!)

Use 1 or 2 sentences for each.

EXAMPLE:

Give us an example of when you have had to take charge under pressure?

S - When I worked as a supervisor at the bistro. One afternoon suddenly became very busy, when an unexpected works party came in.

T – It was important to keep the customers happy, and to ensure that the team was able to cope with the sudden workload.

O – I immediately delegated tasks for each team member, which involved us splitting up in to two groups: serving and preparation of orders. I kept up team morale by setting an example of excellent customer service, while remaining relaxed, focused, and enjoying a few laughs with the customers along the way.

R – This resulted in the staff enjoying the surge in activity, and contributing to the customers being very happy with the level of service.

Y – I believe this shows that I can take charge, comfortably, under pressure.

AT THE INTERVIEW

Take all of your necessary documents with you. Be on time – if necessary stay the night before and make a dummy run so that you know where it is. (I know of somebody that turned up late and, naturally, didn't get the job.) Make sure that you are smart and presentable. Absolutely no jeans or trainers!

Appear confident and do not slouch. Have a firm handshake, maintain eye contact and smile!

Do not waffle and remember to pause, think and then answer (even if you know the answer). Speak clearly.

If you don't know the answer, ask for clarification before telling them that you do not know.

Be polite to *all* members of staff; they may ask one of them what they thought about you! Remember that they all want you to pass, be yourself.

BE ENTHUSIASTIC

Practice the following questions. Think carefully about, and find *your* best answer to, each question. Write in the guide in pencil to help you prepare for the question. I also recommend that you rehearse the answers out loud, to help sound natural when at the interview. Keep yourself calm, keep it relevant and be sensible! Don't dig a hole for yourself.

REMEMBER TO PAUSE, THINK AND THEN ANSWER

- Tell us about yourself.
- Have you any previous convictions?
- What has made you change career?
- Give an example from your past where you persuaded someone to see things from your point of view?
- Give an example of a time when you had to meet a deadline?
- Give an example of witnessing poor standards of work. How did you react? How did they react to what you said? What was the outcome?
- Not including the information on your CV, tell us a little bit about yourself?
- Tell us about an occasion when you placed the cultural needs of others ahead of your own?
- How would you motivate and inspire others to work?
- When have you had to be cost efficient but still achieve the goal?
- Give an example of when you had to show compassion and empathy towards others?
- Give an example of a mistake you have made when working and what you did to prevent it happening again?
- How do you see our business strategy changing in the future? How do you see us achieving this change?
- How do you deal with someone that has a different attitude towards work than you do? Give us an example?
- How do low cost long haul operators affect our business?
- Give an example of when something has not gone to plan and talk us through the steps you took to fix the problem.
- Give an example of when you worked on a project without guidance.
- Tell us about when you have improved customer service.
- Give an example of when you have demonstrated leadership skills.
- Give an example of when you have worked effectively in a team.
- Why do you want to be a pilot and what skills and qualities would you bring to the role?

- What are the pros and cons of working for our Airline?
- Give an example of a team decision you made at work that others haven't liked.
- Tell us about a plan that has worked badly and one that has worked well.
- Give an example of where you have had to lower your standards at work.
- Give an example of when you have had to take a step back to avoid getting too involved in someone else's problems.
- Give an example of when you have had to pass on difficult news that's non-emotional.
- What do you think multi-cultural diversity brings to an Airline?
- What made you want to be a pilot?
- Tell us about a crisis you have faced.
- How did you fund your training?
- Tell us of a time when, emotionally, you became involved in something that didn't directly affect you.
- Give us an example of when a team has had a good impact.
- You seem like an enthusiastic person, give an example of when your enthusiasm has been dented.
- What has been your biggest ambition accomplished to date?
- On a scale of 1 – 10 how tolerant and intolerant do you think you are?
- Give an example when team morale has been low. What did you do as team leader?
- Tell us about when you have had to deal with confrontation in the team.
- Sum up CRM in one word.
- Define customer service?
- What makes a good pilot?
- What makes you angry?
- What is your opinion with regard to "bending the rules"?
- When have you bent the rules to meet an objective?

- Give an example of when you have taken a risk.
- Give an example of when you have led by example.
- Others in a team have made a decision that you disagree with, how do you deal with this?
- Give an example of when you have failed in an area at work.
- Give an example of when you have done something well.
- Tell us about a time when you have had to change a decision.
- When have you improved customer service?
- Tell us about a bad-flying experience you have had.
- How can we as pilots make an airline more efficient?
- How can aircraft manufacturers make an airline more efficient?
- What makes you laugh?
- What do your friends say about you?
- What makes a good FO?
- What are the main business issues affecting our airline at the moment?
- What do you like about flying?
- Do you break rules?
- Define operating procedures.
- What major events have happened to XYZAIR on a European level in the last two years?
- What has been XYZAIR's policy over the last 2 years? Do you agree with it?
- What will be your final goal at XYZAIR?
- With your previous leadership/management experience how do you think you will cope being an FO with fewer responsibilities than in your previous role(s)?
- How can XYZAIR improve our fuel efficiency?
- How do you see your career progressing?
- Do you view cultural diversity as being important?
- How do you ensure in your work that you are culturally aware?

- Do you set yourself high standards? How do you know when you've achieved them?
- Can you give an example of when SOP's should not be followed?
- What has been your biggest challenge to date?
- Give an example of when you have had to persuade somebody to tell somebody else bad news
- Give an example of when you have been sensitive to the needs of others.
- What are your expectations of XYZAIR?
- When have you had to be sensitive to a situation? How did you go about it?
- Out of everyone we interview today, why should we employ you?
- Give an example of a team situation where the team has ignored your idea.
- Tell us of a time when you have had to take over the lead.
- On a scale between traditional and liberal views, how traditional do you believe you are?
- Give us an example of an occasion where you have been drawn into a conflict and how you dealt with it?
- How would you get a team member back on side if they were ready to leave?
- When have you had to work on a project without guidance? How did you make sure that the team remained focused?
- What would you do if a procedure exists that you don't agree with?
- How is the current market for pilots?
- What are the names of our chairman and CEO?
- What is our share price this morning?
- You make a remark to a captain, which is ignored. What would you do?
- Others in the team have decided a course of action, which goes against your beliefs and morals. How do you cope?
- You've been in a lot of teams; there must have been a time when you fell out with somebody?

- When have you had to build a relationship with people?
- What is the toughest personal goal you have ever set for yourself? How did it work out?
- When have you had to get another member of your team to make an unpopular decision?
- What are the flight crew considerations when flying to Russia?
- What is the current price of a barrel of oil?
- What are the financial issues facing XYZAIR at the moment?
- Why do you want to work for XYZAIR?
- What will you bring to us at XYZAIR?
- Give us an example of when you have had to push the boundaries to complete a job.
- What are our routes?
- How do we differ from our immediate competitors?
- When did you ever go "outside the box" to solve a problem?
- Do you mind how long it will take to become a captain?
- What will be your main challenges when you start flying for an airline?
- How do you recognise when you have had too much?
- Do you ever feel the need to slow down or speed up the way you work on the flight deck?
- How do you adapt to a working practice that you disagree with?
- What would be your hardest challenge if you were to work for us?
- Give an example of a time when you have been crucial to a team. What was your approach to the team and how did you deal with the demands of the team?
- If you got the job with us, what goal or objective would you set for yourself?
- You made a professional mistake. How would you handle it?
- Give an example of when you were too accommodating within the team?
- What makes you passionate about XYZAIR and what sets us apart from other airlines?

- When have you ever disappointed yourself and explain how it changed you.
- How can a pilot add to customer service?
- What makes you adaptable?
- Is there anything you dislike about being a leader?
- What do you enjoy about being a leader?
- What is your biggest ambition in life?
- Give an example of when you have been in a challenging situation. Is there anything you would have done differently?
- Give an example of when you made a very important decision.
- How do you share your plans and mental models with others?
- Give an example of when you resolved a misunderstanding at work.
- Give an example of when you have "gone the extra mile" for a team or for a customer?
- How can we at XYZAIR improve our fuel efficiency?
- What would your school friends say about you?
- How do you think pilots can secure the long-term future of XYZAIR?
- Do you ever break the speed limit? So you are willing to break the law driving, what's to stop you doing so when flying?
- Give an example of when you have had to deal with an awkward situation.
- Give an example of when you could have done something better.
- Describe a complex situation you have been in.
- Give an example of when you were forced to make someone see your point of view.
- What issues do you see XYZAIR facing in the future?
- What do you think of the XYZAIR uniform?
- Give an example of when you have been under pressure and how did you deal with it? What was the outcome?
- What are your views on feedback?
- Give an example of when you have given feedback.

- Give an example of when you have received feedback.
- Give an example of when you made an important contribution to a team.
- Give an example of when you have failed to achieve a goal or target.
- Give an example of when you have set and achieved a goal or target.
- When have you had to get involved with someone else's emotional problems?
- When have you had an issue over cultural diversity?
- Give an example of when you had to back out of a commitment you have given to others.
- Give an example of when you have been in a team which has been more concerned about intra-relationships than the task.
- Tell us of a time you have had to weigh up the benefits to yourself against the cost of someone else.
- Tell us of a time you have had to weigh up the cost to yourself against the benefits of someone else.
- Have you ever had to support a team member who was unable to perform?
- How do you know when you are getting overloaded?
- How do you recognize if you've been under pressure? How does it manifest itself?
- Name a few advantages and disadvantages of SOP's.
- Should SOP's be questioned? If so when?
- Give an example of when you didn't agree with something and how did you deal with it?
- Tell us of a time that you have been under pressure when flying. How did you feel and how did you cope?
- Tell us of a time when you have been in a group and have had an issue with another member which turned out to be an issue with cultural diversity. How did the problem affect other group members?
- Give an example of a time when you have had to recover from giving poor customer service.

- Whenever you take a risk, how do you asses the risk beforehand?
- Give us an example of when you exercised bad judgment.
- Give us an example of you exercising bad judgment when you were under pressure.
- How do you deal with criticism? Can you give us an example of when you have been criticised?
- Please explain why communication is an important component of CRM.
- Tell us of a time when you have had to maintain an interest in something, even if it did not live up to your expectations.
- What makes you tick?
- What are the characteristics of a good Captain?
- What are the characteristics of a good FO?
- Were there any difficulties you faced during your flying training?
- Why is CRM important and what are its benefits?
- How can flight crew motivate cabin crew?
- You're having a technical problem, what is your strategy in solving that problem?
- How do you motivate other team members?
- How do you delegate work to other team members?
- Explain a dramatic change in your life. How did you cope with it?
- Explain an example of when you have been in a really heavy situation and when things have got really serious.
- What help or support did you receive with your flight training?
- What would you do if you if you see a cabin crewmember being annoyed by your captain whilst on a night stop?
- What would you do if you smelt alcohol on your captains' breath?
- What was your first solo like?
- What if you forgot your licence and you were the standby crew?
- You have 2 work related tasks. How do you go about ensuring each one receives the time and attention to detail that it deserves?

- You have been working on a single task for some time. How do you keep the momentum going?
- At DA you judge that the captain doesn't have sufficient visual reference, and he continues his approach. What would you do?
- You are on the ground and have just missed your gate. How would you recover?
- Tell us about when you have had to be assertive and make your point.
- Give us an example of when you have had a problem with a customer.
- What would you do if your captain was exceeding the speed restriction for that level or on an approach?
- What are the key elements of successful communication?
- Which of your qualities would you like to develop further?
- When have you been in a team situation and not agreed with the team leader? How did you deal with it?
- How can XYZAIR improve customer satisfaction?
- Does cultural diversity have a role to play on the flight deck?
- Give an example of when you have influenced others?
- What impact would you have on XYZAIR?
- Give an example of a time when you improved customer service.
- Give an example of when you have taken a risk.
- Who in XYZAIR can help with your training?
- What is the current financial status of XYZAIR?
- During training did anyone annoy you? If so why?
- What was your lowest point when you were training?
- Give an example of when you have made a good decision?
- Give an example of when you have made a bad decision?
- Where do you see your career in 10 years from now?
- Give an example of when you have dealt with cultural diversity.
- Give an example of a breakdown in communications and how you solved the problem.
- How do you cope under pressure?

- What will be your final goal with XYZAIR?
- Give an example of when you have not met your own expectations.
- Give an example of when you have not met the expectations of others.
- Give an example of when you have had to remove yourself from a team in order to meet a goal.
- Give an example of when you have dealt with change. How did this make you feel? Did you have problems adapting?
- Give an example of how you have intervened to solve conflict/ confrontation of others.
- What did you least enjoy about your last job?
- How could you contribute towards customer relations, as a pilot?
- Give an example of when you made a decision under pressure.
- What do your friends say about you?
- You see your Captain drinking just outside the 8 hours before a flight, what would you do?
- You see your Captain drinking within the 8 hours before a flight, what would you do?
- Do you break rules?
- Give an example of when you have had to use an original idea to solve a problem.
- Give an example of when you had to lead a team that really didn't want to do a task.
- Why did you choose XYZSCHOOL for your training? In hindsight would you have done anything differently?
- Give an example of when there was a change of procedure at work. How did you cope with this?
- How would I, as a Captain, know that you are in a high workload situation?
- What improvements have we been making in the cabin at XYZAIR?
- Who makes up the team required to turn around an aircraft? What role do the cabin crew play?
- What was the worst decision you made in your life and how did you overcome it?

- Who are the most important people you should be nice to, as a pilot, in order to help your day run smooth?
- Give an example of when you have had to push the boundaries to get the job done?
- When have you built a relationship with someone outside of a team to get the job done?
- What are the major issues affecting the aviation industry today?
- Tell me about XYZAIR?
- Talk about a time when you have gone through a bad stage in your life, with nobody there to help or guide you.
- Talk about a time where a team have made a decision and ignored your ideas.
- Give an example of when there appeared to be a problem that turned out to be a cultural diversity related issue.
- Ignoring terrorism and fuel prices – what problems face us, specifically, at XYZAIR, and what are we doing about them?
- Give us an example of when you took on someone else's problem? How did you cope?
- Give an example of when you have had to maintain an interest in something, even if it didn't live up to your expectations.
- During the last 6 months when have you had to delegate something to someone?
- What is your strategy for dealing with a technical problem, flying or otherwise?
- Are there any social situations in which you don't feel comfortable?
- Give an example of a time when you made a critical decision that went wrong.
- Which practices in your previous work did you not agree with?
- What is good communication?
- Why are XYZAIR so different to other Airlines?
- How would you make XYZAIR even better?
- Tell us about a recent time when you were faced with a complex situation, how did you deal with it?

- Tell us more about your hobbies and interests.
- What are your strengths and weaknesses?
- Who else have you applied to?
- What would you do if they also accept you?
- Tell us about your family history.
- Are you a good pilot?
- Do you have a good sense of humour?
- Which of our routes are most profitable?
- What are your views on drinking and driving?
- What will you do if you are not successful?
- When did you first become interested in flying?
- What is your style of leadership?
- Which aspect about yourself would you most like to change?
- What were your highs and lows?
- Who is the "team"?

PREPARE YOUR OWN QUESTIONS.

The interview is a two way process! You will be expected to ask questions of your own. It will show that you have prepared for the interview. Be sensible about the questions you ask though. Don't dive in asking about salary, perks, leave entitlement etc. They will usually give you this information during an orientation at the start of the interview. Ask if you must, but leave it until last.

Ideal questions would be something like:

- What are the opportunities for career advancement within XYZAIR?
- Assuming that I'm successful today – what happens next in the selection process? And when will it take place?
- When will I know the outcome of the interview?
- Can I be debriefed on this interview?
- How long, on average, does it take to become a captain with XYZAIR?

CHAPTER 4
PSYCHOMETRIC TESTING

During nearly every Airline selection process these days you will be required to complete several Psychometric Tests. Richard McMunn, the director of How2become Ltd, has kindly supplied some sample psychometric tests, which you will give you a good idea.

His website **www.how2become.co.uk** has thousands of these types of questions that can be practiced online. I recommend that you go there to practice as often as possible, leading up to your interview/assessment.

WHAT ARE PSYCHOMETRIC TESTS?

Psychometric Tests comprise: Ability Tests and Personality Tests and are a measure of general intelligence, attainment, aptitude, personality, attitudes, interests, values and motivators. They assess you against the Airline Pilot job requirements in terms of knowledge, skills, experience and personality.

There are over fifty human abilities, which fall into four categories:

- Cognition (verbal or numerical reasoning)
- Psychomotor (hand-eye co-ordination)
- Sensory (hearing, touch, taste, smell, sight)
- Physical (stamina and strength)

The main tests measure cognitive reasoning and are typically:

- Verbal
- Numerical
- Perceptual
- Spatial
- Abstract
- Mechanical

Practice the following tests under timed conditions to see how you do.

VERBAL ABILITY TEST

During this part of the test you will be required to answer 30 questions in 9 minutes, which equates to an average of approximately 18 seconds per question. This test is designed to assess your English language skills. The test is multiple-choice in nature and in the real test you will have 5 options to choose from. The most effective way to prepare for this type of test is to practice sample questions under timed conditions. Other ways of improving your ability include carrying out crosswords, word searches or any other tests that require an ability to work with the English language. You may also decide to purchase your own psychometric test booklet, which can be obtained from all good websites including www.how2become.co.uk.

Take a look at the following sample question.

Sample question 1

Which of the following words is the odd one out?

A. Spanner   **B.** Pliers   **C.** Hammer   **D.** Brush   **E.** Drill

The answer is D – Brush. This is because all of the other items are tools and the brush is an item used for cleaning, therefore the odd one out.

Now take a look at the next sample question.

Sample question 2

The following sentence has one word missing. Which word makes the best sense of the sentence?

He had been ...... for hours and was starting to lose his concentration.

A. studying   **B.** sleeping   **C.** complaining   **D.** walk   **E.** targeting

The correct answer is A – studying, as this word makes best sense of the sentence.

Now try verbal ability exercise 1 that follows. There are 30 questions and you have 9 minutes in which to complete them.

VERBAL ABILITY TEST 1

Question 1

Which of the following words is the odd one out?

A. Car   **B.** Aeroplane   **C.** Train   **D.** Bicycle   **E.** House

Answer [   ]

Question 2

Which of the following is the odd one out?

A. Right   **B.** White   **C.** Dart   **D.** Bright   **E.** Sight

Answer [   ]

Question 3

The following sentence has one word missing. Which word makes the best sense of the sentence?

The mechanic worked on the car for 3 hours. At the end of the 3 hours he was . . . .

A. Home   **B.** Rich   **C.** Crying   **D.** Exhausted   **E.** Thinking

Answer [   ]

Question 4

The following sentence has 2 words missing. Which two words make best sense of the sentence?

The man . . . . to walk along the beach with his dog. He threw the stick and the dog . . . . it.

A. hated/chose   **B.** decided/wanted   **C.** liked/chased
D. hurried/chased   **E.** hated/loved

Answer [   ]

Question 5

In the line below, the word outside of the brackets will only go with three of the words inside the brackets to make longer words. Which ONE word will it NOT go with?

A	B	C	D
In (direct	famous	desirable	cart)

Answer [   ]

Question 6

In the line below, the word outside of the brackets will only go with three of the words inside the brackets to make longer words. Which ONE word will it NOT go with?

A	B	C	D
In (decisive	reference	destructible	convenience)

Answer [   ]

Question 7

In the line below, the word outside of the brackets will only go with three of the words inside the brackets to make longer words. Which ONE word will it NOT go with?

A	B	C	D
A (float	bout	part	peck)

Answer [   ]

Question 8

Which of the following words is the odd one out?

A. Pink   **B.** Salt   **C.** Ball   **D.** Red   **E.** Grey

Answer [   ]

Question 9

Which of the following words is the odd one out?

A. Run   **B.** Jog   **C.** Walk   **D.** Sit   **E.** Sprint

Answer

Question 10

Which of the following words is the odd one out?

A. Eagle   **B.** Plane   **C.** Squirrel   **D.** Cloud   **E.** Bird

Answer

Question 11

Which of the following words is the odd one out?

A. Gold   **B.** Ivory   **C.** Platinum   **D.** Bronze   **E.** Silver

Answer

Question 12

Which of the following is the odd one out?

A. Pond   **B.** River   **C.** Stream   **D.** Brook   **E.** Ocean

Answer

Question 13

Which of the following is the odd one out?

A. Wood   **B.** Chair   **C.** Table   **D.** Cupboard   **E.** Stool

Answer

Question 14

Which three letter word can be placed in front of the following words to make a new word?

Time   Break   Light   Dreamer

Answer [   ]

Question 15

Which four letter word can be placed in front of the following words to make a new word?

Box   Bag   Age   Card

Answer [   ]

Question 16

The following sentence has one word missing. Which ONE word makes the best sense of the sentence?

After walking for an hour in search of the pub, David decided it was time to turn . . . . and go back home.

A. up   **B.** in   **C.** home   **D.** around   **E.** through

Answer [   ]

Question 17

The following sentence has one word missing. Which ONE word makes the best sense of the sentence?

We are continually updating the site and would be . . . . to hear any comments you may have.

A. Pleased   **B.** Worried   **C.** Available   **D.** Suited   **E.** Scared

Answer [   ]

Question 18

The following sentence has two words missing. Which TWO words make the best sense of the sentence?

The Fleet Air Arm is the Royal Navy's air force. It numbers some 6,200 people, ... is 11.5% of the . . . . Royal Naval strength.

A. which/total   **B.** and/total   **C.** which/predicted

D. and/corporate   **E.** which/approximately

Answer [   ]

Question 19

The following sentence has one word missing. Which ONE word makes the best sense of the sentence?

The Navy has had to . . . . and progress to be ever prepared to defend the British waters from rival forces.

A. develop   **B.** manoeuvre   **C.** change   **D.** seek   **E.** watch

Answer [   ]

Question 20

Which of the following is the odd one out?

A. Cat   **B.** Dog   **C.** Hamster   **D.** Owl   **E.** Rabbit

Answer [   ]

Question 21

Which word best fits the following sentence?

My doctor says I . . . . smoke. It's bad for my health.

A. will   **B.** wouldn't   **C.** shouldn't   **D.** like   **E.** might

Answer [   ]

Question 22

Which word best fits the following sentence?

The best thing for a hangover is to go to bed and sleep it . . . .

A. through   **B.** over   **C.** away   **D.** in   **E.** off

Answer [ ]

Question 23

Complete the following sentence:

By the time Jane arrived at the disco, Andrew . . . .

A. hadn't gone   **B.** already left   **C.** has already Left

D. had stayed   **E.** had already left

Answer [ ]

Question 24

Which of the following words is the odd one out?

A. Lawnmower   **B.** Hose   **C.** Rake   **D.** Carpet   **E.** Shovel

Answer [ ]

Question 25

Complete the following sentence:

Karla was offered the job . . . . having poor qualifications.

A. although   **B.** even though   **C.** with   **D.** without   **E.** despite

Answer [ ]

Question 26

Complete the following sentence:

Not only . . . . to Glasgow but he also visited many other places in Scotland too.

A. did she   **B.** did he   **C.** did he go   **D.** she went   **E.** she saw

Answer [   ]

Question 27

Complete the following sentence:

Now please remember, you . . . . the test until the teacher tells you to.

A. shouldn't   **B.** will not be starting   **C.** are not to

D. can't   **E.** are not to start

Answer [   ]

Question 28

Which of the following is the odd one out?

A. Strawberry   **B.** Raspberry   **C.** Peach   **D.** Blackberry   **E.** Blueberry

Answer [   ]

Question 29

Which of the following is the odd one out?

A. Football   **B.** Wrestling   **C.** Table tennis   **D.** Golf   **E.** Rugby

Answer [   ]

Question 30

Which of the following is the odd one out?

A. Man   **B.** Milkman   **C.** Secretary   **D.** Police Officer   **E.** Firefighter

Answer [   ]

ANSWERS TO VERBAL ABILITY TEST 1

1.	E	**16.**	D
2.	C	**17.**	A
3.	D	**18.**	A
4.	C	**19.**	A
5.	D	**20.**	D
6.	B	**21.**	C
7.	D	**22.**	E
8.	D	**23.**	E
9.	D	**24.**	D
10.	C	**25.**	E
11.	B	**26.**	C
12.	A	**27.**	E
13.	A	**28.**	C
14.	Day	**29.**	B
15.	Post	**30.**	A

NUMERICAL REASONING TESTS

This type of test is used to determine how accurately you can carry out numerical addition, subtraction, division, multiplication and also interpret numerical information such as charts, graphs and tables. The test will also assess your ability to use fractions, decimals and different formulae. As you can imagine, the most effective way to prepare for this type of test is to carry out lots of sample numerical reasoning test questions, without the aid of a calculator.

During the actual numerical reasoning test that you will be required to sit you will have a specific amount of time to answer each question. It is important that you do not spend too much time on one particular question. Remember that the clock is ticking. Have a go at the first numerical reasoning exercise that follows and use a blank sheet of paper to work out your calculations. Remember to check your answers very carefully. It is important that you check any incorrect answers to see why you got them wrong.

You have 10 minutes in which to answer the 20 questions. Calculators are not permitted.

NUMERICAL REASONING TEST 1

Question 1

Calculate 5.99 + 16.02

A. 19.01   **B.** 20.01   **C.** 21.99   **D.** 22.99   **E.** 22.01

Answer

Question 2

Calculate 3.47 – 1.20

A. 22.7   **B.** 2.27   **C.** 1.27   **D.** 2.67   **E.** 0.27

Answer

Question 3

Calculate 98.26 – 62.89

A. 37.35   **B.** 35.37   **C.** 36.35   **D.** 36.37   **E.** 37.73

Answer

Question 4

Calculate 45.71 – 29.87

A. 14.84   **B.** 18.88   **C.** 14.89   **D.** 15.84   **E.** 15.85

Answer

Question 5

Calculate 564.87 + 321.60

A. 886.45   **B.** 886.74   **C.** 886.47   **D.** 868.47   **E.** 868.74

Answer

Question 6

Calculate 16.0 – 9.9

A. 6.9   **B.** 6.1   **C.** 7.1   **D.** 7.9   **E.** 5.1

Answer [   ]

Question 7

Calculate 1109.12 + 0.8

A. 1109.20   **B.** 1109.92   **C.** 1109.02   **D.** 1110.20   **E.** 1110.92

Answer [   ]

Question 8

Calculate 4.1 × 3.0

A. 123   **B.** 9.1   **C.** 12.41   **D.** 7.1   **E.** 12.3

Answer [   ]

Question 9

Calculate 16.8 × 4

A. 67.2   **B.** 64.8   **C.** 64.47.1   **D.** 67.4   **E.** 67.8

Answer [   ]

Question 10

Calculate 2.2 × 2.2

A. 4.4   **B.** 44.4   **C.** 2.84   **D.** 4.84   **E.** 8.44

Answer [   ]

Question 11

In the following question what is the value of *t*?

$$\frac{5\,(t - 32)}{2} = 5$$

Answer [   ]

Question 12

In the following question what is the value of *t*?

$$\frac{3\,(t + 35)}{6} = 35$$

Answer [   ]

Question 13

In the following question what is the value of *t*?

$$\frac{9\,(t \times 16)}{5} = 144$$

Answer [   ]

Question 14

In the following question what is the value of t?

$$\frac{9\,(t \times 16)}{5} = 144$$

Answer [   ]

Question 15

Convert 0.7 to a fraction

A. $\dfrac{7}{10}$ **B.** $\dfrac{3}{4}$ **C.** $\dfrac{75}{1}$ **D.** $\dfrac{1}{10}$ **E.** $\dfrac{2}{3}$

Answer [ ]

Question 16

Convert 2.5 to a fraction

A. $\dfrac{25}{1}$ **B.** $\dfrac{3}{6}$ **C.** $2\dfrac{1}{2}$ **D.** $\dfrac{1}{25}$ **E.** $2\dfrac{2}{1}$

Answer [ ]

Question 17

Convert 3.75 to a fraction

A. $\dfrac{75}{1}$ **B.** $\dfrac{1}{375}$ **C.** $3\dfrac{1}{75}$ **D.** $\dfrac{75}{3}$ **E.** $3\dfrac{3}{4}$

Answer [ ]

Question 18

Convert $\dfrac{3}{10}$ to decimal

A. 3.0   **B.** 0.3   **C.** 3.33   **D.** 0.03   **E.** 0.003

Answer [ ]

Question 19

Convert $\dfrac{1}{4}$ to decimal

A. 0.025   **B.** 2.5   **C.** 0.25   **D.** 0.4   **E.** 4.0

Answer [   ]

Question 20

Convert $\dfrac{4}{5}$ to decimal

A. 0.08   **B.** 8.0   **C.** 4.5   **D.** 5.4   **E.** 0.8

Answer [   ]

ANSWERS TO NUMERICAL REASONING TEST 1

1.	E	11.	D
2.	B	12.	A
3.	B	13.	E
4.	D	14.	D
5.	C	15.	A
6.	B	16.	C
7.	B	17.	E
8.	E	18.	B
9.	A	19.	C
10.	D	20.	E

SPATIAL REASONING TESTS

The definition of spatial reasoning is as follows:

'The ability to interpret and make drawings from mental images and visualise movement or change in those images.'

Let us take a look at a sample question.

EXAMPLE QUESTION

Take a look at the following 3 shapes. Note the letters on the side of each shape:

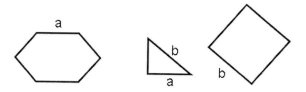

Join all of the 3 shapes together with the corresponding letters to make the following shape:

During the following spatial reasoning exercise your task is to look at the given shapes and decide which of the examples matches the shape when joined together by the corresponding letters. You have 3 minutes to answer the 8 questions.

SPATIAL REASONING TEST 1

Question 1

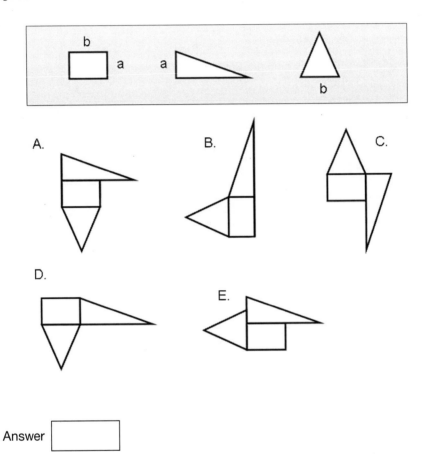

Answer [   ]

Question 2

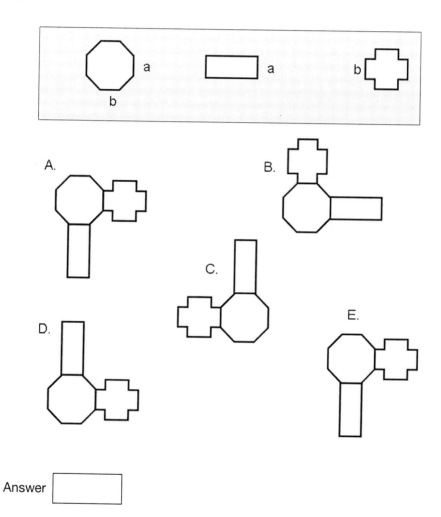

Answer [   ]

Question 3

A.

B.

C.

D.

E.

Answer

Question 4

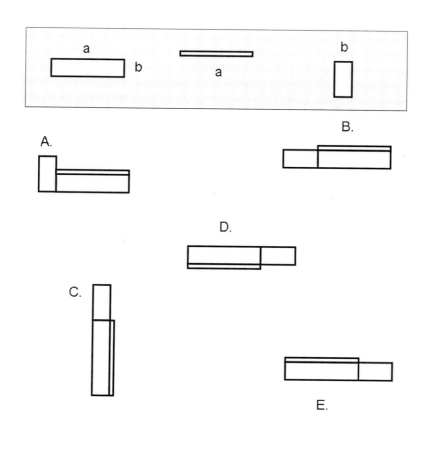

Answer [   ]

Question 5

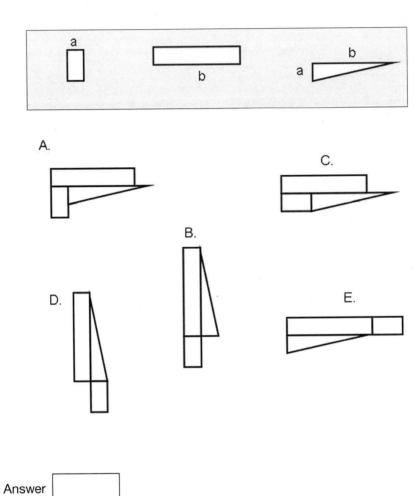

Answer

Question 6

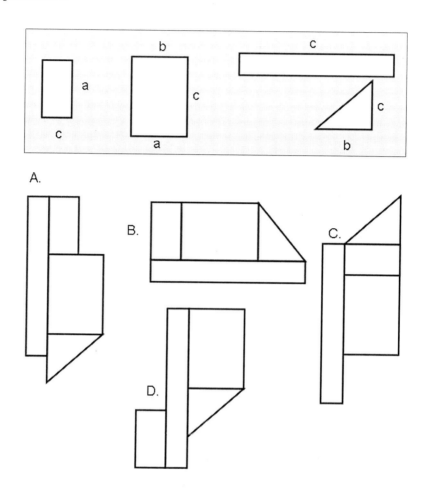

Answer [   ]

Question 7

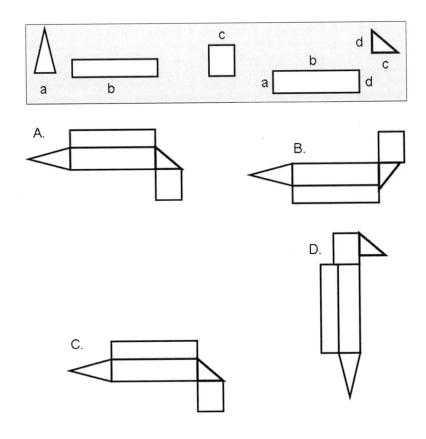

Answer ☐

Question 8

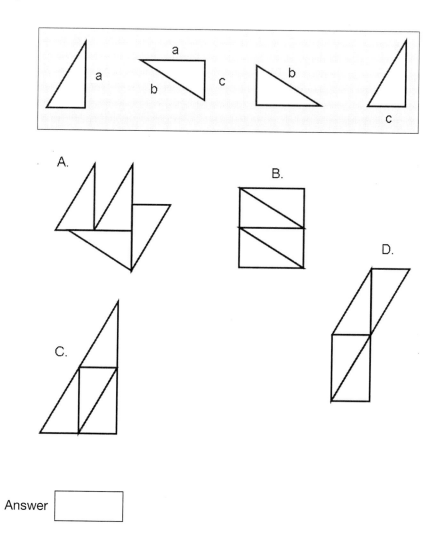

Answer ☐

Now that you have completed the exercise take the time to work through your answers carefully. If you got any incorrect, make sure you understand how the correct answer is reached as this will assist you during your development.

ANSWERS TO SPATIAL REASONING TEST 1

1. B

2. D

3. A

4. E

5. D

6. B

7. A

8. C

MECHANICAL COMPREHENSION TESTS

Mechanical comprehension tests are an assessment that measures an individual's aptitude to learn mechanical skills. The tests are usually multiple choice in nature and present simple, frequently encountered mechanisms and situations. The majority of mechanical comprehension tests require a working knowledge of basic mechanical operations and the application of physical laws. On the following pages I have provided you with a number of example questions to help you prepare for the tests. Work through them as quickly as possible but remember to go back and check which ones you get wrong; more importantly, make sure you understand how the correct answer is reached.

In this particular exercise there are 20 questions and you have 10 minutes in which to answer them.

MECHANICAL COMPREHENSION TEST 1

Question 1

If Circle 'B' turns in a Clockwise direction, which way will circle 'A' turn?

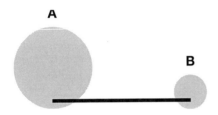

A. Clockwise

B. Anti-Clockwise

C. Backwards and forwards

D. It won't move

Answer

Question 2

Which square is carrying the heaviest load?

A. Square A

B. Square B

Answer

Question 3

Which pendulum will swing at the slowest speed?

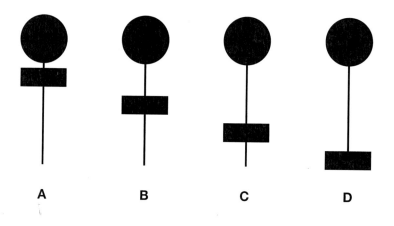

Answer ☐

Question 4

If Cog 'A' turns in an anti-clockwise direction which way will Cog 'B' turn?

A. Clockwise

B. Anti-Clockwise

Answer ☐

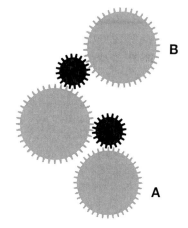

Question 5

If Cog 'B' moves in a clockwise direction, which way will Cog 'A' turn?

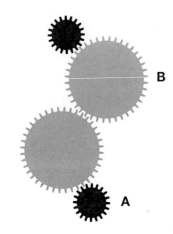

A. Clockwise

B. Anti-Clockwise

Answer _____

Question 6

Which shelf can carry the greatest load?

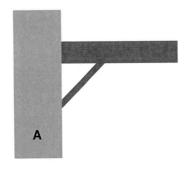

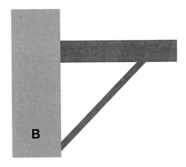

A. Shelf A

B. Shelf B

Answer _____

Question 7

At which point will the pendulum be travelling at the greatest speed?

A. Point A

B. Point B

C. Point C

Answer [   ]

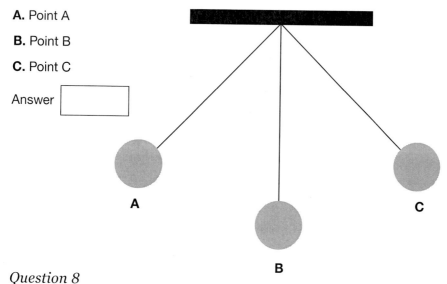

Question 8

At which point will the beam balance?

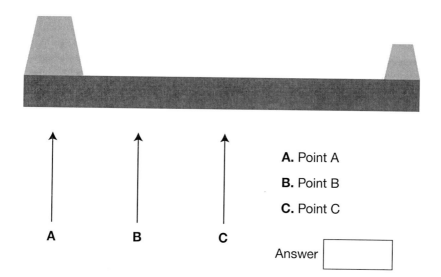

A. Point A

B. Point B

C. Point C

Answer [   ]

Question 9

If water is poured into the narrow tube, up to point 'X', what height would it reach in the wide tube?

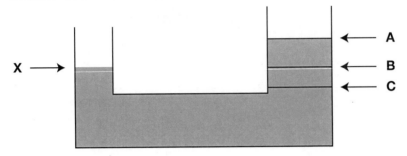

A. Point A

B. Point B

C. Point C

Answer

Question 10

At which point would Ball 'Y' have to be at to balance out Ball 'X'?

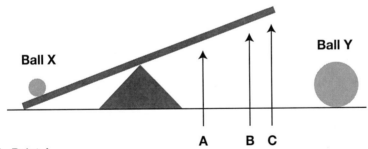

A. Point A

B. Point B

C. Point C

Answer

Question 11

If Cog 'A' turns anti-clockwise, which way will Cog 'F' turn?

A. Cannot say

B. Clockwise

C. Anti-Clockwise

Answer [   ]

Question 12

Which post is carrying the heaviest load?

A. Both the Same

B. Post X

C. Post Y

Answer [   ]

Question 13

If water is poured in at Point D, which tube will overflow first?

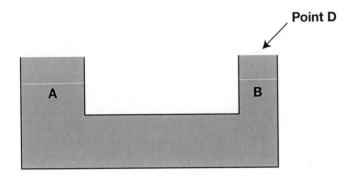

A. Tube A

B. Both the same

C. Tube B

Answer

Question 14

At which point would it be easier to haul up load X?

A. Both the Same

B. Point A

C. Point B

Answer

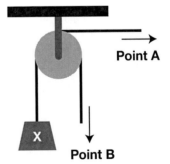

Question 15

If rope 'A' is pulled in the direction of the arrow, which way will wheel 'C' turn?

A. Clockwise

B. Anti-clockwise

C. It will not turn

Answer

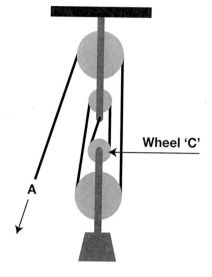

Wheel 'C'

A

Question 16

Which load is the heaviest?

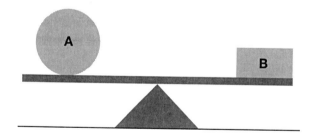

A. Both the Same

B. Load B

C. Load A

Answer

Question 17

If rope 'A' is pulled in the direction of the arrow, which direction will Load 'Q' travel in?

A. It will not move

B. Down

C. Up

Answer

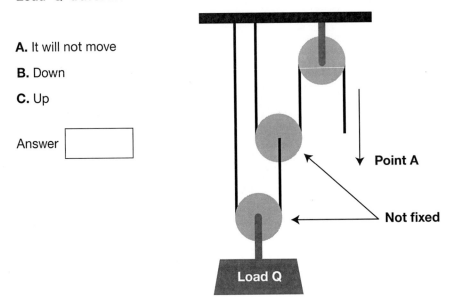

Question 18

If circle 'X' turns anti-clockwise, which way will circle 'Y' turn?

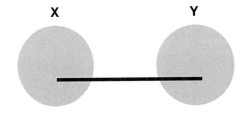

A. Anti-clockwise

B. Clockwise

C. Backwards and forwards

Answer

Question 19

Which pulley system will be the easiest to lift the bucket of water?

A. Both the Same

B. Pulley A

C. Pulley B

Answer

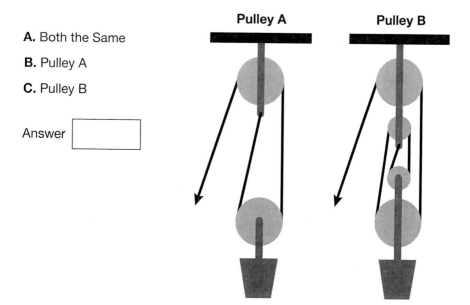

Question 20

At which point(s) will the pendulum be swinging the fastest?

A. Point 1

B. Points 1 and 5

C. Points 3 and 5

D. Point 3

Answer

ANSWERS TO MECHANICAL COMPREHENSION TEST 1

1. C
2. B
3. D
4. B
5. A
6. B
7. B
8. B
9. B
10. A

11. C
12. A
13. B
14. B
15. B
16. A
17. C
18. A
19. C
20. D

PERSONALITY TEST

These tests gauge your personality by asking about your feelings, thoughts and behaviour in a variety of situations.

Depending on the duration of the test, you may need to answer between 50-250 statements.

You will have to answer each one on a scale of 2, 5 or 7. (i.e. 1 being not like me, and 5 being exactly like me)

Here are some examples:

- Do people who are inefficient anger you?
- Do you like to first plan a task?
- If you are criticised before others, do you feel bad?
- Do you prefer to avoid arguments?
- Do you prefer to do a task alone?
- Do you care what others think of you?
- Do you prefer facts?
- Do you donate to charity regularly?
- Do you feel more comfortable doing one job at a time?
- Do you gain pleasure from trying to make sense of the meaning of art and poetry?
- Are you affected if one of your friends are in trouble?

Then there are simple **a)** or **b)** type answers:

I prefer to avoid conflict.

    a) True   **b)** False

ANOTHER STYLE OF PERSONALITY QUESTIONNAIRE:

I enjoy parties and other social occasions.

    a) Strongly disagree

    b) Disagree

    c) Agree

    d) Strongly agree

    e) Neutral

Work is the most important thing in my whole life.

a) Very strongly disagree

b) Strongly disagree

c) Disagree

BAgree

e) Very strongly agree

f) Strongly agree

g) Neutral

APTITUDE TEST

This is a computer-based test and normally lasts around 90 minutes.

The test covers:

- Hand-eye co-ordination
- multi-tasking
- memory test
- situation awareness
- mental arithmetic

The aptitude test will also include the Psychomotor Test. You will be shown into a room and sat down at a computer with a joystick. The test will measure your ability to make sense of information in two dimensions, so as to achieve a solution in a three-dimensional form.

Using your joystick you have to position a dot onto a pattern, which is moving in a random manner on the screen, as it scrolls down. At the same time, you are required to control the "rudder" of the plane with your feet. This task is designed to evaluate if you have the ability to complete several tasks at once. Therefore, the longer you can position the dot on the set pattern, the higher your score will be. In the final analysis, the test determines whether you have the natural aptitude to fly an aircraft.

THE PSYCHOMOTOR TEST PROFILE

As I mentioned above, you will be seated in front of a desktop computer with a joystick. You will also have a mouse and mini keyboard. The test composes of 5 parts:

1. There will be a static cross at the centre of the screen and you'll have to control two lines (vertical & horizontal) with your joystick. To move the horizontal line you must either pull the joystick back or push forward. For the vertical line, you move it either left or right. Because of the virtual 'wind factor', the two lines will be moving continually.

   The aim is to steer the two lines together so that they will both come to be upon the static cross. This test consists of three parts. All three parts of the test are similar and the scores range from 1 – 10 for each part of the test.

2. This is a test of your observation. Here, you'll have to wear a set of headphones and use the mini-keyboard as the main input device. You'll get three men standing in four positions (facing you, back facing you, upside down facing you, and upside down back facing you).

   Each of them are holding either a round or square object in each of their hands. Then, a voice from your headphones will ask you how many of them are holding either a round/square object on which hands. Your answer would be either all three of them (keypad number 3), two of them or one of them, or it could even be none of them. This test has a time limit.

3. Once again, for this test, you'll be using the mini-keyboard as the main input device. You'll get two very untidy diagrams and you are given an 'X' shape at the bottom. For each area of the test you will have to define whether the 'X' shape could be found on the 1st diagram or the 2nd diagram, or even both of the diagrams. You'll have a time limit of 30 seconds.

4. For this test you will be using the mouse to click on the objects. You'll be given a table of co-ordination. There are around five or six rows and five or six columns each. The rows represent the colours and the columns represent the shapes. For this test, there are two similar

parts. It should be noted that, the rows of colours, and columns of shapes are constantly changing.

5. For this test, you'll be using a joystick again. Believe it or not, you'll be virtually flying an aircraft! The only thing is you will have to fly into the trail of boxes that are coming towards you. This test composes of three parts and the score ranges from 1 – 10.

Top Tip: *Move the joystick GENTLY.*

MEMORY TEST

The memory test evaluates the short-term memory and tolerance for stress. This is a test of your ability to detect relevant information, whilst being distracted by similar but irrelevant information. This is the kind of thing which can typically occur in a cockpit environment.

The above tests are good examples; go to **www.how2become.com** and practice lots of them. The more practice you do, the better you will become.

You should try to find out a better idea of the tests you will be sitting on the day by using **www.pprune.com**. I guarantee that somebody on the forum will have already done them and posted feedback.

CHAPTER 5
THE TECHNICAL INTERVIEW

As already mentioned in the guide, for the technical interview section I strongly recommend that you invest in the following books:

- *Ace The Technical Pilot Interview* by Gary V Bristow,
- *Preparing For Your Cathay Pacific Interview by Captains XY and Z,* (Questions from this book are used by several Airlines) and
- *Handling The Big Jets* by DP Davies.

Following are plenty of typical Technical Interview questions to give you an idea of what to expect:

Q. *Why are T-Tails and Propellers prone to icing?*

A. Smaller Surface/Thinnest Aerofoils.

Q. How does weather radar work?

A. Primary radar source emits pulsed signals in the SHF band, often using doppler techniques to detect water molecules suspended in the atmosphere. The size and type of molecule, will determine the type of return. Phased array antennas receive the returns and this is displayed to the pilots by colour coded displays.

Q. Can you describe the formation of a cumulonimbus cloud?

A. Warm moist air suddenly lifted. High relative humidity airmass which is forced to rise either through oragraphic relief, frontal or by large heat source, ie convectional. This humid airmass must be rising in an unstable atmosphere (once lifted, it will continue to rise as it remains hotter than the ambient conditions). This gives rise to tall cloud formations, containing large up and down currents, often containing large super cooled water droplets. Often only top out at the tropopause.

Q. What is the Tropopause?

A. Atmospheric boundary between troposphere and stratosphere.

Q. What is a Microburst?

A. A microburst is a small, very intense downdraft that descends to the ground resulting in a strong wind divergence. The size of the event is typically less than 4 kilometers across. Microbursts are capable of producing winds of more than 100 mph causing significant damage. The life span of a microburst is around 5-15 minutes.

Q. What is Advection Fog?

A. Advection fog is the fog that is produced when damp air is moved across a surface that is cooler than the air. It is most commonly seen over seas or other bodies of water.

Q. Describe the advantages and disadvantages of rear mounted overhead engines, and under-slung pod engines.

A. Undeslung pods:

+ Design allows a wider range of engines to be fitted due to lying close to the airframe c of g (Not a large moment arm).

+ Reduced wing bending. Potential to increase the MZFW

+ Engine pylon acts as a wing fence to reduce spanwise flow

- Closer to FOD and potential for ground contact.

- Power pitch couple

Overhead engines:

+ Reduced power pitch couple

+ Less critical if a fire occurs due to distance from fuel tanks

+ Less chance of FOD ingestion and ground contact.

+ Clean wing

- Limited airframe design due to the large moment arm (trim sensitive).

Q. Describe the advantages and disadvantages of fuselage mounted engines and under-slung pod engines.

A. As above.

Q. What is the purpose of winglets? Why doesn't the B777 have them?

A. A winglet acts just the same as a wing fence. It aims to reduce the spanwise flow which ultimately gives rise to induced drag. If you reduce induced drag, this will reduce the total drag of an aircraft and so we burn less fuel. The B777 achieves the same result but by using a raked wing. This is a higher swept portion of the wing, found close to the tip with high aspect ratio

Q. What are Vortillons?

A. Small fencelike surfaces extending in front of the wing and attached to the undersurface. They are particularly useful in preventing spanwise flow at high angles of attack. Often they are found ahead of control surfaces to improve control effectiveness by drawing in fast flowing air into the boundary layer.

Q. What is the wingspan of the (XYZAIR type of aircraft)?

A. XYZ meters!

Q. I see that you did your IR on the PA34. Can you describe its electrical system?

A. 2 × 65 amp alternators, 12 volt 35 ampere-hour battery etc....

Q. What is EGPWS?

A. Enhanced Ground Proximity Warning System - Uses feeds from the radio altimeter and also an internal database, to give crews time to respond to impending ground contact.

Q. What is TCAS?

A. Traffic Collision and Avoidance System. Secondary radar based system. Will give traffic alerts or resolution advisories where applicable. Can only advise crew to make vertical corrections. These are both aurally and visually annunciated and more importantly always with respect and opposite to both aircraft.

Q. What is RVSM?

A. Reduced Vertical Separation Minima. Between FL290 - FL410 - keeps aircraft 1000ft vertically separated to give higher traffic volumes flowing.

Q. What is the purpose of swept wings?

A. Delay the drag rise caused by compressibility near the speed of sound due to bow waves.

Q. Describe "coffin corner"?

A. The altitude at or near which a fixed wing aircraft's speed is equal to the critical mach number, at a given gross weight and g-force loading.

Q. What do you need to consider when flying from warmer air into colder air at a constant indicated altitude?

A. Effect of temperature on altitude. When air is warmer than average, you are higher than your altimeter indicates. When temperature is colder than average, you are lower than indicated. When flying from warm to cold air at a constant indicated altitude, you are losing true altitude.

Q. What is the endurance of the PA34?

A. 4 Hours.

Q. How many fuel tanks are fitted to the PA34?

A. 2 (sometimes fitted with optional bladder tanks to make 4 total)

Q. What are the vital actions for a PA34 engine fire?

A. 'Engine Fire no. 1/2 Engine" Fuel selector off, throttle close, prop feather, mixture I.C.O. Firewall close etc....

Q. What would you do if the anti–icing system was struggling to cope with severe icing?

A. Immediately start working to get out of icing conditions

Q. You are flying with an experienced Training Captain who does not respond at DA when you say "Decide" What would you do?

A. Take Control. Assertively stating, "I have control" if visual land if not go around!

Q. What are the pros and cons of "fly-by-wire"?

A. Pros - allows aircraft to be designed more statically and dynamically unstable which reduces drag and improves total efficiency.

Pros - Airframe limits can be designed not to be reached by incorporating system logic to prevent incorrect pilot input.

Cons - expensive to maintain and keep up to date.

Q. What are Rake Wingtips?

A. Reduce drag and increase fuel efficiency. See B787 dreamliner.

Q. How do you plan for icing conditions?

A. Avoid as best as possible

Q. Describe the Anti-Icing system on (XYZAIR's aircraft type)

A. XYZ

Q. What are the flap settings on the XYZTYPE?

A. XYZ degrees

Q. How does the fuel cross feed work on the PA34? When would you use it?

A. See P.O.H

Q. What icing conditions is the PA34 certified to?

A. See P.O.H.

Q. Tell me about the hydraulic system on the PA34?

A. See P.O.H

Q. Describe induced drag?

A. Aerofoils can produce wake vortices. These cause a downwash which in turn increases with high angles of attack. This means induced drag increases with high angles of attack. Induced drag is a by-product of lift.

Q. Describe profile drag?

A. Drag due to motion of a body through the air (or fluid) Made up of skin drag, form drag and interference drag.

Q. What are the advantages of a turbofan engine?

A. Fuel efficiency, less noise etc.

Q. Describe windshear?

A. Sudden variation of wind over either horizontal or vertical distances.

Q. Airbus or Boeing? Why?

A. Personal preference?

Q. I see you also have lots of hours on the PA28. When is carb' ice most likely to form?

A. A warm day with high humidity

Q. How do flaps affect the take off roll?

A. Increase drag, but lower Vr and V2 resulting in shorter TODR.

Q. What is meant by a "high by-pass ratio"?

A. Turbo fans direct air both into and around the core of it's engine. When a higher proportion of the total airflow is directed around as opposed to into the core, this is a high by pass ratio.

Q. How does GPS work?

A. 29(24 with 5 spares) satellites all in separate orbits, 4 required for position and altitude, use trilateration to determine position.

Q. What is AHRS?

A. Attitude and heading reference system. A system composed of three-axis sensors that provide heading, attitude, and yaw information for aircraft. AHRS are designed to replace traditional mechanical gyroscopic flight instruments and provide superior reliability and accuracy.

Q. Where do swept wings stall first and why?

A. At the tip due to the induced span wise flow of the boundary layer from root to tip

Q. What do you think of the A380?

A. Answer questions like this sensibly!

Q. What is the Mach number ratio?

A. Mach Number = TAS/LSS

Q. What is the equation for lift?

A. L=CL ½R S V²

Q. What are the main differences between light aircraft and a Boeing 757/767?

A. Much greater Speeds, much greater weight/momentum, trim range, handling characteristics. (See *Handling the Big Jets* by D.P. Davies)

Q. What is the purpose of spoilers?

A. Dump lift and increase drag during landing roll.

Q. What are slats and why are they used?

A. Slats are aerodynamic surfaces on the leading edge of the wings which, when deployed, allow the wing to operate at a higher angle of attack. A higher coefficient of lift is produced as a result of angle of attack and speed, so by deploying slats an aircraft can fly at slower speeds, or take off and land in shorter distances. They are usually used while landing.

Q. Your TAS is 300kts, HWC 60kts on your outbound leg. You fly out for one hour. How long is the return journey?

A. Your groundspeed outbound is 240kts. If you travel for 1 hr you are 240 nm away. On return you travel at 360 kts to cover 240nm. This will take 40 mins.

Q. You fly a circling approach to the reciprocal runway, you then have to go around on short final. How do you carry out the missed approach procedure?

    A. Climbing turn towards the missed approach procedure.

Q. What is Mcrit?

    A. A Mcrit is the speed of an aircraft at which some point of the structure has air flowing at Mach 1. This is usually on some point of an aerofoil where airflow is accelerated.

Q. When planning a descent at standard speeds in an airliner that's light, would you plan to descend earlier or later than if it were heavy? Why?

    A. At a standard airspeed (say 250 knots) a heavier aircraft will have a higher angle of attack, which will in turn increase the gliding range. Conversely, at the same speed a lighter aircraft requires a lower angle of attack, which will decrease the gliding range. Therefore when lighter descend later, and when heavier descend earlier.

Q. What factors influence Vref?

    A. Usually 1.3 times Vs and is affected by Cl max and weight.

Q. What is meant by percentage MAC?

    A. Imagine that the MAC (Mean Aerodynamic Chord) on a particular airplane is 100", and the CG falls 20" behind the leading edge of the MAC. That means it falls one-fifth of the way back, or at 20% of the MAC.

Q. What is meant by the "specific gravity" of fuel?

    A. The ratio of the mass of fuel to the mass of an equal volume of distilled water at 4°C (39°F)

Q. You upload 1000 litres of fuel with an SG of 0.8. How many kilogrammes of fuel have you just uploaded?

    A. 1000(litres) × 0.8(sg) = 800(kg)

Q. At 10,000 ft you commence a constant descent profile. What's your required ROD(Rate of Descent) if you have 20 mins to run?

    A. 500fpm (feet per minute) Depends on groundspeed.

Q. Describe ground effect?

A. Ground effect refers to the increased lift and decreased drag that an aircraft wing generates when an aircraft is about one wingspan's length or less over the ground. Ground effect often gives pilots the feeling that the aircraft is "floating", especially when landing.

Q. What is the "black hole effect"?

A. Approaching a runway at night, under conditions with no lights before the runway and with city lights or rising terrain beyond the runway. These conditions may produce the visual illusion of being too high on final approach, resulting in pitching the aircraft nose down to decrease the perceived approach angle.

Q. What are FADECs?

A. Full Authority Digital Engine Control

Q. What is the ceiling of the XYZTYPE?

A. Flight level XYZ

Q. What does an inverter do?

A. Converts DC electricity to AC electricity

Q. What is Mach Tuck?

A. Once the boundary layer separates from a swept wing as it goes supersonic, the centre of pressure moves rearwards (root to tip on a swept wing) causing a nose down pitching moment.

Q. What are Mach Trimmers?

A. It artificially corrects for tuck above mcrit by sensing the speed and signaling a proportional upward movement of the elevator or variable incidence tailplane. It maintains pitch attitude throughout its speed range up to the aircrafts max Mach demonstrated diving speed (MDF).

Q. You are ICAO classified as a "light" aircraft. How many miles separation do you require from an ICAO classified "Heavy" aircraft on final approach?

A. 6 Nautical Miles.

Q. What is a deep stall or "superstall"? Which aircraft design is susceptible to this and what system prevents it?

A. Aircraft with a T-tail configuration. In these designs, the turbulent wake of a stalled main wing "blankets" the horizontal stabilizer, rendering the elevators ineffective and preventing the aircraft from recovering from the stall. Stick shakers and stick pushers are fitted to prevent this.

Q. After a PA34 Engine Failure. How would you balance your fuel?

A. Crossfeed.

Q. What happens to the centre of pressure as the aircraft reaches Mcrit?

A. It moves rearwards span wise from root to tip.

Q. What is aquaplaning? What is the Aquaplaning speed formula?

A. Standing water causes the moving wheel of an aircraft to lose contact with the surface on which it is load bearing with the result that braking action on the wheel is not effective in reducing the ground speed of the aircraft. The formula is 9 x the square root of the Tyre pressure in Psi.

Q. Explain Dutch Roll?

A. A "dutch roll" is a type of aircraft motion, consisting of an out-of-phase combination of "tail-wagging" and rocking from side to side. The response of the aircraft to a disturbance from equilibrium is a combined rolling/yawing oscillation in which the rolling motion is phased to precede the yawing motion. The yawing motion is not too significant, but the roll is much more noticeable. When the aircraft rolls back toward level flight in response to dihedral effect, it rolls back too far and sideslips the other way. Thus, the aircraft overshoots each time because of the dihedral effect of the wings. Yaw dampers prevent it.

Q. Explain Adverse Yaw?

A. Results from an aileron deflection and a roll rate, such as when entering or exiting a turn. It is called "adverse" because it acts opposite to the yaw moment needed to execute the desired turn.

When initiating a turn the adverse yaw comes from wings' lift vectors opposing, from aileron profile drag and greater induced drag on the up going wing. It's removed with coordinated rudder control.

Q. What is a yaw damper?

A. It has yaw rate sensors and a processor that provides a signal to an actuator connected to the rudder. It prevents Dutch Roll.

Q. What is hardover protection?

A. This feature is applicable in the case of a runaway rudder. If deflection is greater than a certain angle and pedal force the system shuts off the hydraulic rudder systems and they revert to manual control (Manual reversion) i.e. Emb 135/145.

Q. What is the advantage of a variable incidence tailplane?

A. The tailplane or the horizontal stabilizer, used either by itself or in addition to a trimming tab, in which the incidence can be varied to balance out-of-trim forces. This arrangement is more effective than trim tabs at high Mach numbers. Easier for trimming a large range of speeds, therefore more fuel efficient due to less drag.

Q. What are roll control spoilers?

A. Primarily fitted to reduce adverse yaw when rudder input is limited by higher speed. They are raised on one wing, thus decreasing lift and increasing drag, causing roll and yaw. Sometimes fitted in combination with or in lieu of ailerons.

Q. How does an Aft C of G affect stalling speed?

A. Stalling speed decreases as the C of G moves aft as less negative lift is required from the tail and the aircraft is aerodynamically lighter. While the benefits of an aft C of G is a lower stall speed, the adverse result of an aft C of G is less stability as there is less elevator authority.

Q. What is speed stability?

A. Straight and level airspeeds above the minimum drag speed for the current conditions are considered stable speeds. The faster the speed gets beyond minimum drag speed the faster it reverts after a disturbance. At all speeds slower than minimum drag speed, the speed will continue to decrease if decreased by a disturbance. (The back end of the drag curve)

Q. What are the differences between a propeller aircraft and a jet aircraft when landing?

A. Approach speeds, momentum, response to power/thrust demands, landing distance required. See Handling the big jets by D.P.Davies.

Q. What is spiral stability?

A. To be spirally stable, an aircraft must have some combination of a sufficiently large dihedral, which increases roll stability, and a sufficiently long vertical tail arm, which increases yaw damping. Increasing the vertical tail area then magnifies the degree of stability or instability

Q. What is dihedral? What is anhedral?

A. Angle of the wing from root to tip. Dihedral angled upwards to increase stability. Anhedral angled downwards to decrease stability.

Q. How does a turbofan engine work?

A. Cold air enters the fan and bypasses the engine core at typically 10 parts to 1. Air that goes through the core passes through a low-pressure compressor then through a high-pressure compressor heating the air to a very high temperature. The hot air enters the combustion chamber where it is mixed with fuel, ignited and drives the turbine on a concentric shaft to the fan, LP and HP compressors. The cold air and hot gas mix at the exhaust increases propulsion and reduces noise.

Q. What are variable inlet guide vanes?

A. These are normally in front of the first stage of an axial compressor and sometimes in the subsequent stages as well. Inlet guide vanes can be changed to meet the requirements of the engine-operating conditions. Their purpose is to prevent compressor stall by making sure the compressor blades are fed air at the correct angle of attack for the engine speed.

Q. What's the difference between holding above or below FL140?

A. Below FL140 outbound time 1 minute. Above FL140 outbound time 1 minute 30 seconds (ICAO)

Q. You are currently the Pilot Flying. You are in the approach stage, flying level at 7000ft on the destination airfield's QNH 1030. Your colleague failed to reset his altimeter subscale from 1013. What does his altimeter read?

A. 1030 – 1013 = 17 Hpa (hectopascals).

1 Hpa = 30 ft (approx)

17 Hpa × 30 ft = 510 ft

Your colleague's altimeter will read 510ft *lower* than yours 6490ft. On noticing the error he would have to wind his altimeter subscale up from 1013 to 1030 to indicate 7000ft on his altimeter.

This should give you a good idea of the type of technical interview questions you will get asked. You may also be set a technical questionnaire/written paper (usually multi-choice) with similar questions. Now I'll give you an example of a typical simulator assessment.

CHAPTER 6
THE FLIGHT SIMULATOR ASSESSMENT

I need to mention here that each simulator assessment is different. However, this profile will serve as a guide and useful tool, to help you be prepared as to what to expect at your assessment.

*I must point out that the following information doesn't represent any particular aircraft and has been completely made up in order to give you an **idea** of a typical simulator assessment.*

This part normally lasts about an hour.

Remember, the goal of the airline is to see how flexible you are in adapting your skills to something new – they want to see that you will be able to get through the type rating course.

Be aware that the airline may conduct the simulator in an aircraft that they don't fly themselves. They will watch how you brief the approach; how you cope with mistakes (and how you learn from them). They will be looking for a high standard of Instrument Flying. Your scan must be nice and sharp for this.

Handy Tips:

At the briefing, take a deep breath, compose yourself, and listen carefully to the instructions given. Don't miss out on important numbers, speeds, power settings and such like. If in doubt, ask the assessor.

BE WELL PREPARED

Contact me (ONLY WHEN YOU HAVE A SIM' ASSESSMENT PLEASE) at the email address: **frozenatpl@aol.co.uk**. I will then provide you with details of a simulator preparation course that I recommend you undertake.

It will massively help your chances if you do! Use Microsoft Flight Sim' to help your scan. There is an add-on for virtually every type of aircraft now. Use RANT Radio Aids Navigation Tutor, to revise holds etc.

A TYPICAL SIMULATOR ASSESSMENT

The XYZAIR simulator assessment will incorporate the following exercises:

- General handling
- Take-off and climb
- Radar vectored ILS to land.
- Engine failure during flight
- One engine inoperative ILS to land

The XYZ Aircraft simulator will be flown from the right hand seat.

The flight director and auto-throttle will not be used.

The training captain who completes this assessment will occupy the left seat and will act as a competent Pilot Not Flying (PNF). He will NOT provide any training input, but he will answer any questions you have before starting the detail. He will not debrief you at the end of the session.

AIRCRAFT CONTROLS

STEERING

Rudder pedal steering provides control throughout the initial part of the takeoff and latter stages of the landing run.

TRIMMERS

All aircraft trim controls are electric. The horizontal stabiliser trim switches are on the outboard part of the control wheel.

AIRSPEED INDICATOR

The analogue airspeed indicator includes a digital readout. There is 1(orange) internal airspeed cursor and 4 (white) external bugs. Selecting the required speed onto the mode control panel operates the orange cursor – this will be done, on command, by the PNF.

ELECTRONIC ATTITUDE INDICATOR (EADI)

The EADI is a standard presentation. Bank angle is indicated at the top of the EADI and is graduated in 10-degree increments. Thirty degrees of bank is to be used for turning manoeuvres. Pitch graduations are labelled every 15 degrees, sub-divided every 2 degrees. A speed tape is located to the left of the attitude display.

MFD MULTI-FUNCTIONAL DISPLAY

The Multi-Function Display (MFD) presents radar, TCAS, FMS, CMC and other navigation information and systems pages.

ALTIMETER

A conventional altimeter is fitted with a moveable index to bug decision altitude.

VERTICAL SPEED INDICATOR (VSI)

The VSI is a standard presentation. Indications are derived from the inertial reference system so that the readout is instantaneous.

RADIO MANAGEMENT UNIT (RMU)

The Radio Management Unit consists of a display and a bezel panel that provides control of the communications and radio navigation equipment. Additional airplane systems information is also available on specific RMU selectable pages.

FLIGHT DETAIL

You will board with engines running and before takeoff checks completed. The aircraft will be positioned at the threshold of runway 23R at Manchester. You can expect a brief familiarisation of the flight deck instrumentation.

Takeoff and climb thrust is 86% N1.

You will be cleared for takeoff and climb initially on runway heading to 4000 ft. Ask for takeoff thrust to be set and maintain the runway centre-line with rudder pedal control.

At Vr rotate at 3 degrees per second to 16 degrees, and with a positive rate of climb call "gear up."

Climb at V2+15 kts to 1000 ft agl and then lower the nose to 11 degrees to give a climb rate of not less than 1000 fpm.

With a speed in excess of V2+15 kts, flap retraction is initiated by calling "flap Zero."

Passing 170kts then accelerate to clean manoeuvring speed.

A short general handling exercise to include turning, climbing and descending will follow the take-off.

You will then be radar vectored towards the localizer for runway 23R at 215 kts and it will be up to you to determine the best point to reduce speed. Ultimately, you will be cleared for an ILS and landing on runway 23R. The following flap manoeuvring speed schedule must be followed for deceleration:

Beginning at the manoeuvring speed of 200 kts, extend flaps to the next setting. As the flaps extend, reduce speed to 180 kts.

Flap 45 is used for a two-engine landing. And Flap 22 is used for one engine inoperative landing.

Reduce speed to 180 kts before establishing on the localiser. Approaching the glideslope, reduce speed to be fully configured for landing as descent commences.

Following the landing you will be repositioned final approach with both engines operating. An engine will fail and you will be required to maintain control.

To counteract overall thrust reduction, BOTH thrust levers should be advanced. To control thrust asymmetry due to engine failure, smooth rudder application is required. Finally, the rudder load is trimmed out.

The rudder is very powerful. Avoid over controlling on the rudder as the yaw will cause roll and induce pilot control wheel input. The slip indicator below the PFD must be used to maintain zero aircraft yaw.

The final requirement is to fly a one engine inoperative ILS and landing.

For a real simulator assessment – with a real aircraft type! There would be diagrams and clear examples of the profiles flown, along with thrust and attitude settings. Again you would have tables or diagrams clearly illustrating these. There would also be clear diagrams of the instruments.

CHAPTER 7
GROUP EXERCISES

In this exercise the group takes part in three exercises:

1. Practical problem solving

2. Group discussion

3. Communication and verbal reasoning.

The exercises generally last half a day, with two assessors monitoring the group closely.

A typical group discussion question could be:

- How could high fuel prices affect your career as a pilot?

- How would it be possible to change the traditional image of an airline pilot?

The group could also be set various challenges:

- Discover the best method to drop food aid parcels to villages in need, via the most fuel-efficient route. Also take into account packing the goods, so that they leave the aircraft in order. Think about volume of packages etc.

- Build a bridge out of pieces of wood that could hold a cup of water.

The group would also be given exercises that test their verbal reasoning. Here are three examples:

- You find yourself stuck on an island. What items do you think would be essential for you to have with you?

- Discuss together a typical issue in the news and reach a conclusion.

- Build a bridge that would be able to support a glass of water.

Bear in mind, the assessors are looking for team skills such as listening, questioning for clarity and making statements clearly.

There is no need to worry about achieving a realistic solution. Be aware that the assessors are on the lookout for:

- Leadership

- Decisiveness

- Enthusiasm

- Positive and supportive attitude

- Energy

Each group member will be graded on a scale from "well below average" to "well above average."

Your personal style, task skills and team skills are assessed.

Personal Style – Manner i.e. calm cheery etc. level of involvement, supportive and cooperative, easy to work with and constructive reasoning.

Task Skills – goal oriented, positive contribution, time aware, admit errors and respond accordingly, understand the briefing.

Team Skills – good listener, clarify, seek/give support, seek/give ideas, take the lead/make decisions, question, speak clearly.

Top Tip: Make sure that you don't try to dominate, argue or point score.

Try hard to give a positive contribution to the discussions and above all, get to know your team, relax and enjoy it!

CHAPTER 8
ONLINE RESOURCES

AVIATION JOBS

www.just4aviation.net

www.aviationjobsearch.com

www.flightinternational.com

www.ppjn.com

www.coffeelovesmilk.com

www.bestaviation.net

PILOT UNIONS

www.ipapilot.com

www.balpa.org

AIRLINE PARTNERSHIPS

www.ctcwings.com

www.oaa.com

www.ftejerez.com

AIRLINE SPONSORSHIP

www.propilot.eu/your-career/west-atlantic-cadet-scheme

www.cathaypacific.com

UK AIRLINE ADDRESSES/AOC HOLDERS

www.caa.co.uk/aocholders

PILOT RUMOURS AND JOB NEWS/FORUMS UK/EU

www.pprune.com

www.pilotjobsnetwork.com

USA

www.airlinepilotforums.com

PSYCHOMETRIC TESTS,
INTERVIEW TECHNIQUES AND TIPS

www.how2become.co.uk

A FEW FINAL WORDS

Use the following "selection day" checklist before you attend:

- Are you fully confident with your non-technical interview answers?
- Have you practiced, and are you fully confident with psychometric tests?
- Have you prepared fully and are you confident with the technical questions?
- Have you practiced the simulator profile through a couple of times?
- Have you prepared, and are you confident how you perform group exercises?
- Have you done your homework on the airline/aircraft?
- Have you prepared your documents and travel arrangements etc.?

If the answer to all of the above is a confident yes, then you will surely get through selection, and will be head and shoulders above most other candidates.

You have now reached the end of the guide and no doubt you will be ready to start preparing for the airline pilot interview and selection process. Just before you go off and start on your preparation, consider the following.

The majority of candidates who pass the interview and selection process have a number of common attributes. These are as follows:

1. **They believe in themselves.**

    The first factor is self-belief. Regardless of what anyone tells you, you can become a pilot. Just like any job of this nature, you have to be prepared to work very hard in order to be successful. Make sure you have the self-belief to pass the selection process and fill your mind with positive thoughts. Be sure to prepare for every question contained within this workbook.

2. **They prepare fully.**

    The second factor is preparation. Those people who achieve in life prepare fully for every eventuality and that is what you must do when you apply to become a pilot with a specific airline. Work very hard and especially concentrate on your weak areas.

3. **They persevere.**

    Perseverance is a fantastic word. Everybody comes across obstacles or setbacks in their life, but it is what you do about those setbacks that is important. If you fail at something, then ask yourself 'why' you have failed. This will allow you to improve for next time and if you keep improving and trying, success will eventually follow. Apply this same method of thinking when you apply to become an airline pilot.

4. **They are self-motivated.**

    How much do you want this job? Do you want it, or do you really want it?

When you apply to join the airline you should want it more than anything in the world. You levels of self-motivation will shine through on your application and during your interview/assessments. For the weeks and months leading up to the selection process, be motivated as best you can and always keep your fitness levels up as this will serve to increase your levels of motivation.

Work hard, stay focused and be what you want...

Lee Woolaston

P.S. If you have enjoyed my guide I would be grateful if you would give me a positive 5-star review on Amazon!

Get more career
guides and interview
preparation products
and services at:

www.how2become.co.uk